Authentically You

EMPOWER YOUR WAY TO SUCCESS

Dr. Julie Ducharme

For information contact:
Dr. Julie Ducharme
www.drjulieducharme.com

Interior and cover design by Joshua Ducharme

ISBN: 978-1-0993-7996-3

Printed in the United States of America.

Dedication

I found my inspiration for this book in the worst way. I thought about this book for years but struggled with the idea of writing about the demons I struggled with. Opening myself up to let others see my imperfections was a tough thought. Then the inspiration came, and sadly, it was not a good inspiration. A beautiful young woman who didn't realize her worth left us all too early in her life. This beautiful young woman could light up a room with her smile and had a genuine soul, took her life. I don't know all the demons she fought, but I do know she never knew her worth and how much she meant to so many people. To her, I dedicate this book, and all women, young and old, who do not know their worth, I hope that this writing provides a way for you to learn to be your authentic self.

To my family and friends:

I want to thank my husband for such an amazing amount of support. I would not be where I am without his support behind me, being my biggest fan, and supporting me every step of the way. To all my family and friends who encouraged me along the way, thank you for loving me and showing me that no matter who I am, I am loved.

Contents

Foreword

"How can I be an authentic leader like you?"

You can't! Absolutely positively do not be a leader like me! You cannot and should not be like me!

As I look into the eyes of the dejected recipient of what seems like a devastating blow to an enthusiastic inquiry, a soul crushing blow of comparison saying that someone cannot measure up to me, how I lead, and what I've done... I smile... and ask, "do you think you can be the authentic you, if you're trying to be me?"

Absolutely do not be a leader like me, own *YOU*!

To truly be an authentic leader, you have to own that what makes you different, actually makes you special. So that means, do not be me, or anyone else.

Now, slow down.

Don't worry, I did not just tell you to jump off the leadership cliff with no parachute. What I'm saying is listen, observe, develop, and create your own formula for bringing the best out of people.

Own your background.
Own your differences as strengths.

Own your brand of crazy.
Own your voice, ESPECIALLY when it's different.

And let each situation coach you, as you coach others. Build bridges. Have conversations. Get to know your people. You cannot help people reach their potential if you don't know where they are, what motivates them, and what their dreams are.

Listening is a part of leading.
Do not be afraid of being wrong.
Laugh often.
Strive for connection & consistency.

As I said before, do not be me, take some of the best of me, then add your own special sauce and be the best of you...

And always always always, surround yourself with the best. I want everyone around me to be better than me at *their* thing.

Iron sharpens iron, so rock with the best.

There is no one size fits all leadership bucket that you can (nor should) pour yourself into. If you try you will always be uncomfortable, and therefore not authentic. Think of it this way, imagine putting on a pair of high heels that are 3 sizes too small and attempting to run a marathon. I don't care if those shoes are Christian Louboutin, I am not going to try and jam my feet in those shoes and run. Those shoes were not made for running, and they were not made for my foot. The only thing that's going to happen is I'm going to hurt myself, and I can guarantee, no one is going to follow in my footsteps!

I promised you earlier that I would not push you off the leadership cliff without a parachute, this book is your parachute. It's a practical tool that will help you shift your focus from awkwardly attempting to check someone else's box, when you have the capacity to design your own. Dr. Julie is a wonderful example of taking the No's she heard & flipping them into NOW I'm going to do this.

At 5'2" I've always been the person who was told what I couldn't, shouldn't, and wouldn't do, and thankfully the one thing I didn't do was listen and prove them right. Think about that for a minute, if you quit because someone else told you that you couldn't do something, you just proved them right! Instead, I listen for why someone says something won't work, then thank them for giving me the roadmap to making it work. Dr. Julie is a prime example of this mentality, though we definitely do not have height in common, we are kindred spirits in individuality.

As a young girl, I remember the struggle to fit in. It took me a long time to shift that thinking. Now I own, why fit in when you can stand up, stand out, speak up, and create change.

I've been the 1/1 and the first many times in my career, with no one to look at and say, I want to be her. And yet, I think not being able to fall back on what was successful for anyone else, actually gave me the courage to tap into myself, my power, my voice, and at the same time to be humble enough to let situations coach me. No one has all the answers, so sometimes questions are where true power lies.

In this book, you will be pushed to look internally for answers, to tap back into the you which may have become a bit lost along the way. To truly be an authentic leader, you have to look honestly at yourself: get real, get gritty, get messy, get honest, get raw, and get uncomfortable.

I can tell you, these things aren't easy, but they are priceless. I can promise you, I'm leaving you in great hands with Dr. Julie, and I am so proud of you for taking this step.

On the move! Let's go!

Dr. Jen Welter
First Female NFL Coach

CHAPTER 1

Authentically You: Empower Your Way to Success

"Some days are so dark I can barely see the light and some days are so bright I wonder how I could have ever lost sight of the light."

—DR. JULIE DUCHARME

I sat in my dorm room, tears streaming down my face as I reflected on the words the professor said to me,

"You are not smart enough to be in college; you should drop out."

Those words hit me like a brick. They stung and shocked me. I had received a full scholarship to play my two favorite sports in college, volleyball, and basketball. My dreams, I thought, were coming true. But yet as I sat there, I couldn't get the image out of my head. I sat speechless and stared at the man who looked at me blankly with no emotion and told me I wasn't good enough. I was a mere 18 years old.

This was the first of many No's I would face on my journey. But this one, the **first** one, stuck with me for more than 10 years. As I earned my Bachelors, Masters, and Doctorate degrees, started three companies of my own, and became a young business professor teaching college at age 23, I kept hearing that man's words over and over again, *"You're not good enough; you're not smart enough!"* The saying, "Sticks and stones will break my bones, but words will never hurt me," is probably the most misleading quote **ever.** Heck yeah, words hurt!

I find it interesting that most of the time we remember more of the negative things that people say to us than the positive things. No matter how many compliments and positive messages I heard, I couldn't shake all of the nasty and cruel words that were said. They were like a splinter in your finger you couldn't pull out. It sat there *day in* and *day out* and began to fester and infect so many other aspects of my life.

As I moved forward in my first 4-year degree, I would be told that I would never make it in the field of communications; I heard that I would never be a speaker or a writer, more times than I could count. By my senior year during my undergrad college years, I was told I was dyslexic, and that's why I wouldn't make it. Countless times from so many people, I heard the reoccurring message that I had no chance of achieving success in the field I was pursuing.

My goal at that time in my life was to make it to the Olympic team for volleyball and then transition into becoming a sports newscaster/journalist. Nothing like trying to swallow those negative comments that I would never be good enough or smart enough or be able to pursue my dreams. Thank the good Lord that I am a very competitive and stubborn woman who did not take No for an answer. I pressed on.

I remember growing up with a mom who was always her authentic self; she didn't care what people thought; she was just who she was. She walked to the beat of her own drum, and she encouraged me to do the same. I remember in middle school, I had to work every summer for my grandparents, and the money I made from them, I used to buy my school clothes. I found all these fun clothes that were bright neon colors, shirts, shorts, and hats (yes, it was the 1980s!). I remember thinking how amazing I thought I looked, and my mom told me I looked great, so she encouraged me to buy those clothes. All those years ago and I still remember feeling so amazing just being me—my authentic self.

If you look back at those pictures, I looked pretty crazy, and I am not even talking about how my hair looked in those pictures (remember I did say it was the 1980s!). I remember thinking, *why wouldn't my mom tell me how ridiculous I looked or encourage me to buy something more in line with what the other kids were wearing*? It wasn't until now that I realized she let me be my authentic self. She saw how at that moment I was beaming with confidence; I was my true authentic self—a moment of feeling beautiful, strong, and happy and that is tough to feel that way in middle school.

As I pushed, crawled, climbed, and broke glass ceilings to get to where I wanted to go, I kept trying to figure out the person I wanted to be when I got there. Fast forward to after college. At this time in my life, there were very few women in business as role models; most of the women I tried to confide in just didn't get it. They were in the right profession for women, and I was not; at least that is what I was told. I was entering "Men only" territory, and I was pretty innocent and naive. When I say innocent, I didn't see color or discrimination, or that women couldn't do something. I was raised that whatever I started, I finished; that was the rule. Following that mantra, the path I began, I would definitely finish.

Let me offer an example of what I started to run into when I first applied for a part-time position as a business professor. I remember the man interviewing me, looked right at me, laughed, and said,

"Sweetheart, the English Department is down the hall; you know women don't do business."

Once again, shocked by his comment, I gathered my items and walked out. I remember sitting in my car crying thinking; *I own my own business. How can he say that; how can they be so ignorant? Will I ever get to do what I love? Will ever get to be who I really want to be? How many more doors do I have to have slammed in my face? How many more people laugh at me and say you're too young to teach, or you're too young to own a business? How many more "Sweetheart" remarks do I need to endure to be taken seriously?*

Fast forward 20 years later, a good friend told me as I was conducting a consulting session with her when I shared I fight daily fears, depression, anxiety, and struggles and body issues, she said she was shocked. She said,

"But you always have it together, you are super successful, and you look amazing. How can you have any struggles? You never look like you are struggling."

I told her yes, I had had all this success, but I am continuing to work on accepting myself as I am. Being happy with who I am—the real me.

At that moment, I realized that I need to share my downfalls more than my successes because other people need to know I am not perfect, even though for quite some time I wanted people to think I was perfect. Trying to live your life like that is tough. I realized being my real authentic self was so much more important and brought so much more joy, success, and happiness in my life than perfect Julie. Perfect Julie was exhausting. I decided to throw out society's handbook for regarding who I should be and who I should look like and start to embrace the true authentic Julie. This means that I don't always have it all together; I will still have low and high days. Yes, my house is not always clean, I don't always have dinner on the table, and my life is not perfect. Don't get me wrong, we can always work to improve our weaknesses, but we cannot improve ourselves if we don't first love and accept ourselves for who we are first and foremost. So how do we beat these false ideas, stereotypes—an ideology that is being said, shown, and pounded into us every day?

My goal in this book is to help guide you in becoming your authentic self. You first have to know the true you, who are you, and the person you want to become. When you can embrace you, then you can see change. Embracing you is not an easy process. I am 42, and I've been trying to embrace *me* for a long time. When you can realize your worth, your beauty, and yes, your downfalls, that is when the healing process can begin. You have to remember; life is never perfect. You will still have struggles, absolutely! We are human; it's our nature, but if I can see my worth as a woman, a mother, a wife, and as a business owner, I am one step closer to becoming my authentic self.

As I grew up, it was my Christian faith that sustained me in the tough times, and still does today. If I didn't have my faith, I'm not sure if I would have made it through those dark times as I tried to find my identity and who I wanted to be as a woman. Choosing the moral high road was not always easy, but I realized I wanted to be what my mom believed I could be—someone with purpose, with a willingness to make change.

My life changed drastically six years ago in 2013 when my mother passed away unexpectedly. I remember as if it were yesterday when my mother was dying in the hospital, as my sister, brother, dad, and I sat around her bed. We talked about funny stories that happened growing up with mom; we talked about what a great mom she was. My brother brought his guitar with him, and we sang her favorite songs to her. As we sat there and talked about her, I saw her true inner beauty. Her beauty wasn't in how she looked, her clothes, or even her success. Her true beauty was shown in her family.

She dedicated her life to being a mother determined to raise three kids who would make a change, give back to the world, and help others. She spent her life giving back. As we reflected on her life as she lay dying, we found joy in the midst of our sorrow and despair. We realized what a beautiful authentic life my mother had lived. We all have our own journeys, some with rocky bumps along the way, and some with outright moments of despair, and then moments of such joy you never knew you could be that happy at that moment.

My mother's life ended much too soon, but her legacy of living an authentic life, embracing who she was and how she loved God, how she loved others, even loving the ones who you don't want to love, and give, and give until it hurts because there is always someone who needs it more than you. In that moment of watching my mom die, I knew the type of woman I wanted to be and what my worth was. When my mom took her last breath, and her spirit left her body, I knew she had no regrets because she lived a life true to who she was.

Throughout her entire life, my mother did not care what other people thought. She moved to the beat of her own drum and helped change the lives of so many people with her gift of loving people. This is what my mom had always told me to be.

"Julie, God made you special, and He has a plan for you. I know you will change the world and be a light."

I knew I needed to embrace who I was—*all of me*.

We all have dreams. We all need moments where we stop and look up from the long hard path we have taken to see that beautiful horizon. Without dreams and goals, life can become dark without purpose to guide you, no light to see at the end of the tunnel. My goal in this book is to help you find your authentic self and understand how to embrace it. As you work through the book, you will see the acronym EMPOWER, which stands for

Examine

Make change

Practice change

Owning your power

Worth

Engage

Reflect

My hope is that these steps will help you move toward embracing your authentic self and start down your own authentic path.

Reflection:

Have you ever had that moment when you were being the best version of yourself and felt so amazing? Have you also had that moment where you were anything *but* your authentic self? You will find that not being your authentic self is exhausting and not very fulfilling.

EXERCISE 1.1

Take a moment to write down your favorite things about your personality. I know we all could easily make a list of the things we don't like about ourselves.

Next, ask your friends and family to list characteristics about you that they love. Embracing your authentic self-starts with recognizing the positive traits you have and hearing why people love those traits you show. Try to list 10.

CHAPTER 2
Examine

Often people ask me what does authenticity really mean? Being authentic is going past the very superficial level. Your conversations are not just light topics but are heart-to-heart, gut-wrenching at times conversations. This is when you will get very honest about who you are and what is happening in your life. Often what you share hurts and is very revealing. You may even confess your issues, doubts, and failures. You may admit your fears, strengths, and weaknesses. It is human nature to wear a mask and keep our guard up and pretend that everything is fine. But this can be demise to becoming your authentic self.

I used to love to watch the show *Biggest Loser* (weight loss reality show). I was always amazed at their transformations of how much weight they would lose and how much work they would put in. As you would watch them weekly, you would see tears, anger, and joy. They would have so much pain during the week while they worked to change their destructive eating habits and learn to deal with other issues in their life. During this process, they transformed not just their bodies but their mindset as well.

Many had to overcome and examine issues they struggled with that contributed to their weight gain. They would dig down deep to discover issues of bad relationships, family, and many other things holding them back. As they examined their issues, they made choices to make change; painful, but necessary. Not all weeks were successful for them. I would watch them work so hard, then get on the scale, and it might show a zero-weight loss or just a pound or two. After working so hard, that result can be quite defeating. The end result brought so much joy as they found their true authentic self, hiding under layers of weight. They very often in this transformation realized who they really were or wanted to be and that to make that happen, they had to make changes in their lives.

If we use this example to guide our examination of who we truly are, we can see how as we look at being our authentic self, there may need to be some transformations in certain areas of our lives. It's not always going to be pretty, easy, or joyful, but just like a caterpillar, we will see beauty come from our transformation of embracing our authentic self. But just like a caterpillar, it takes time to transform; it does not happen in one day but time in the cocoon while the metamorphosis happens. There are several definitions of metamorphosis but I like this one the best, "a change of the form or nature of a thing or person into a completely different one, by natural or supernatural means."

The first step is to examine where you are in your life, what makes you happy, as well as what does *not* make you happy. How do these things contribute or hinder you from moving toward what you feel is your true authentic self? At age 42, when I feel I should be so confident about myself and my appearance, I find such insecurity. I accomplished everything I could ever dream of and more, but yet I still look at myself in the mirror after having two kids and think, *"You are not skinny enough, pretty enough, or good enough; you haven't made it yet. Am I worthy enough to stand on this stage with all the other big speakers? Am I worthy at all of anything?"*

I have said many times in my talks that being your authentic self can be terrifying; it requires both courage and humility. It means that in all those fears and insecurities mentioned above, we have to face them, to be able to embrace them and realize we are human. We are not perfect, but we can love ourselves and love our lives and be the best version of ourselves. This feeling means we are opening ourselves up to rejection and being hurt. It also means we are opening ourselves up to an amazing life of authenticity. This begs the question why anyone would want to take the risk of being authentic.

I know I am not alone when I talk about the demons of self-worth and how I fight them every day to be comfortable in my own skin. As I mentioned earlier, a recent suicide of a friend brought to light the importance that we embrace our authentic self and know that we are good enough as the person we are. I know many of you right now are not embracing your authentic self. You are living a life of survival, making it day-to-day, wondering when your chance will come. If you are waiting for a change to happen, it will only come by putting in the hard work. Change only comes when you want to make a change and embrace what you were really made to do in life.

Very often people say to me,

"I want to do what you do; how can I do that?"

I find that to be a loaded question because my path is my path and what I usually ask people after this question is,

"What do you want to really do in your life? What is your

true passion? You can't live the same life or the same path as me. We are different people with different wants, needs, and passions."

This question usually stops people where they are at, and sometimes even stumps them to think. *"What do I really want?"* Often their response is,

"Nobody has ever asked me what I want."

If you want to live a life that you love, then you first need to examine what your goal is in life. Are you moving in a direction to meet that goal? What is keeping you from moving to the goal? And how can you remove those barriers to get to the goal? Not many people want to take a deep look at their life; often they do not like what they see and not sure they want to put in the work to make a change.

Let me share a good example. I was working with a woman many years ago in a very bad situation. She was in an abusive relationship and called me one night after she had been beaten up by her boyfriend, she had a little baby, and was desperate. We took her in to help her get on her feet; we helped her find a job, get to school, and even gave her a car. We gave her all the tools to be able to walk away from this horrible abusive situation and start a new life. We also put in place some requirements that she had to fulfill to move her to be back out on her own. But in the end, despite everything she was given, her chance to have a better life for her and her child, she chose to go back to the bad neighborhood and to her abusive boyfriend.

I remember being shocked. We gave her everything to be successful, but I realized you could give everyone the key to success, but it takes that person wanting to put the key in, to turn and open that door to a new path. That new path means change and change is scary. It doesn't matter who you are. I have found we all get nervous about change, especially change that is very different to you. You would be surprised at how many people (women especially), let fear of change take them back to the bad situation when salvation and freedom are just a foot away from them. They are not willing to take the one step toward that new freedom because they are fearful and are not willing to put in the hard work needed to make change. So, when that key is given to you, how willing are you to use that key to open the door?

How did I know I wanted to change paths? How did I know I was not embracing my authentic self? For me, it became clear after I had my second child. I moved into what would be considered in my industry a very high and prestigious position, especially at my young age. I thought I had made it. They allowed me to work remotely, so I could care for my newborn. It was what I thought was my dream job.

But as I started the job, I found I was working 60-80 hours a week. I spent a majority of time dealing with conflicts between people and trying to avoid my other female colleagues attempting to sabotage me. It was exhausting. I started losing my hair, losing weight, and having anxiety attacks every time the phone rang. I was getting urinary tract infections because I was not getting up to use the bathroom enough because I was working nonstop. Depression started to set in as my boss day in and day out attacked my character and who I was. She wanted to make sure I knew I was nothing special. It took my doctor saying to me "You're in a toxic job that is affecting your health; you need to change careers, or you are going to have a heart attack."

She was right. I have never been so miserable and unhealthy in my life, and I was only 31. But this was supposed to be the path I was to take. Everyone said this was the logical path for my career. I had made it to this prestigious position, my thought, *"I can't quit; everyone will say they were right. I am too young and do not have the experience to make this work."*

This was not the case at all; it was a bad job, bad people, and certainly not my dream job. The stress of thinking of leaving was even worse. I thought about how everyone would think I was a failure and could not handle myself at that level. I was stressed about the money and how I could find another job fast enough. I was working in a toxic environment; my mind and body were telling me to get out. What do you do when what you thought was supposed to be your lifetime job suddenly turns out not to be?

When I finally decided I had to make a move to leave the position, I remember thinking I was having a mental breakdown. I never in my life had felt anything so devastating and defeating as that moment, and here I was about to walk away from the "dream job". What do you do when suddenly your identity is stripped from you? I have never felt such an emptiness, loss, and fear that I did at that moment. I remember I asked my husband to stay home and help with the kids so I could have one day to pull myself together. Secretly, I was very worried. I had anxiety attacks, depression, I didn't sleep, and I was not eating. I knew this was not healthy and not right, but yet walking away from this hostile, toxic environment was so hard for me to do.

Remember the girl I mentioned above who went back to an abusive relationship instead of choosing a new path? It would have been so easy for her just to take a few steps to a new life. I thought about her and realized that I was willing to stick with what I knew and felt safe in and continue to be mentally abused instead of taking the path to happiness and health. In the medical world, they call this *the Stockholm syndrome* which is "feelings of trust or affection felt in many cases of kidnapping or hostage-taking by a victim toward a captor." It's strange how our brains work. I took my day, cried about it, talked to some very encouraging friends, and then submitted my resignation. That moment in my life was the toughest thing I had ever done. I am a strong woman who never backed down from a challenge and never let people treat me poorly. But that day I felt beat, I felt defeated, I felt lost. I didn't know where to go or what to do. I had just walked away from what I thought was my lifetime career. I realized that in that moment of self-examination, it was very painful because I felt like a failure.

After further examination, I realized I had put my identity in my job and in what other people thought of me. You will never win in life if other people and your job are your identities. Jobs go away, and people will let you down. When you are doing what you love to do and are not doing it for recognition or for people to approve of you, then you can't lose. When and if you have these moments, I encourage you to reach out to your mentor, friends, or tribe you have for support. I reached out to one of my mentors that day, told her that what I was hoping for was that she'd hire me. She couldn't hire me full time, but she told me she would hire me part-time, but she then said to me,

> "Julie you have been playing with your business for quite a while, give yourself some freedom, and build that business into a full-time job, I know you can do this."

This mentor had no idea how that comment changed my life. She was someone I respected and trusted, and if she believed I could do this, then I had to try. She had given me a new goal. I didn't think before this moment that I could get my business running full time and make a lot of money because I was always told women *didn't do business.* At that moment, the competitive, resilient Julie showed up. I had a new mission and a new path.

Please know that change does take time. I didn't become a millionaire overnight. It took time to build my business. I worked part-time teaching and part-time building my business, but I had started down a new path and my true path of being an entrepreneur and empowering people. Today I stand tall, blessed with three successful businesses, an author of several empowerment books, a professional speaker at conferences and more BECAUSE I took that first step to become my true authentic self. Sometimes we have to make a wrong turn to find the right way home.

EXERCISE 2.1

Take an 8.5 x 11 sheet of paper and make two columns. In the first column on the left, I want you to make a wish list of things you want to do but haven't or can't. It can be big or small things in your list.

In the right-hand column, list some of the barriers that keep you from doing those things. Now flip the paper over and make a circle. In the inside of the circle, list all the barriers you feel are stopping you from moving forward with the list of items you want to accomplish from the first column. On the outside of the circle, write the words from the column on the left. Then draw lines from the barriers to the no restriction items you listed on the outside to see what and how many barriers continue to stop you from completing that list. (See example below.)

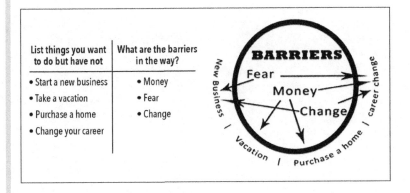

List things you want to do but have not	What are the barriers in the way?
• Start a new business	• Money
• Take a vacation	• Fear
• Purchase a home	• Change
• Change your career	

Next, I want you to journal or talk about how can you remove some of these barriers to bring these things from the wish list to a more realistic list that can be accomplished. Not every barrier will be easy to remove, but you should find that some of these barriers can be changed, moved or adjusted to make some of these items on your wish list a reality. For example, if time is an issue, what can you change to make better use of time? They say we lose 2 hours a day on social media; maybe you give up some social media time to reach your goals?

CHAPTER 3

Making Change

Change is never easy, but necessary!

In our previous chapter, we talked about examining our lives to see what we need to change to become our authentic self. In this chapter, we focus on making the actual change. People on a regular basis say they are going to change... but saying it and actually doing it are two different things. I see a lot of lip service paid to this idea of change, and very little action put into place.

People always ask me what my New Year's resolutions are, but I don't make any because I believe change is constant and needed all the time; I shouldn't wait until once a year to make a change or use the excuse of New Years to make a change. To make the change, you have to change your mindset. I recently watched the TV show *Hoarders* (reality show that helps people clean their hordered houses). I am always amazed at the hoard and the massiveness of it and in particular how the person living in it doesn't see it. One of the main objectives the cleaners, and pyschologist do when they come in and work with theses hoarders is that they can only get them to stop hoarding if they change their mindset. Usually, the person hoarding acknowledges they need to make a change, but they have lived like this for so long they are not always willing to take the next step of making an actual change because change takes work.

Malcolm Gladwell, the author of *Blink,* said it takes 10,000 hours to become an expert. When working on change, all you need to do is start with 30 days of building a good habit. Once you put in those 30 days of change, you are well on your way to those 10,000 hours of being an expert of becoming your authentic self.

If you cannot change your mindset, you cannot embrace your authenticity. Everything you do is motivated by your thought process, to build good habits we need to build in a good thought process as well. A good example is a fast food that is fattening. If I eat too much fast food, I may get fat. The solution? Don't eat a lot of fast food. So why is that my mindset? Because that has been told to me since I was a young child. Now if you suddenly told me that was all untrue and fast food was healthy for me, I would have to work very hard to change my mindset that it was not bad for me. I may have a hard time trusting you because my mindset is programmed to think that. Just know that all your motivation forms from a thought. Your behavior is motivated by the your beliefs, and your attitude prompts your actions.

When we make a change in our life, we can force our-selves to do certain things just like our New Year's resolutions. For example, I want to lose weight, so it will force me to eat less, and exercise more. This mindset can produce short-term solutions, but how often have you set yourself up for something like this and you lasted a week or two, and then your bad habits or mindset kicked back in? Why do people so often fail in making a permanent change in their lives? Because very often, just like my *Biggest Loser* example, people do not want to get to the root cause of what needs to be changed, and you can't make the change if you don't change your mindset.

Because it takes 30 days to make a new habit, and while that may seem like a long time, let's think about the habits we built as a child that we do now without even thinking. For example, brushing our teeth every morning and night is a habit from our very young days. I have done this activity with my kids since they have had teeth. Now they are ages 7 and 10, and naturally, they brush their teeth every morning and night out of habit. I tell my kids over and over, put your dirty clothes in the hamper and they now automatically put it in the hamper and not on the floor. It is situations like this where we make *conscious* efforts over time to have beneficial behavior for our health and well-being.

I always ask people who have habits that are very detrimental to their health, why don't you just stop, in the end, it is going to affect your health severally. They reply that they can't stop, because they are addicted, or many other excuses. But the truth is, we all have the will to stop the behavior that is bad for us, but we have to decide first if that is what we want. I have met people who said I just stopped smoking one day. They realized it was bad and they stopped. Or they just stopped drinking. They didn't want to be that person anymore, and because they wanted to change badly enough to make the effort, they stopped.

So here is my question to you, how badly do you want to change your circumstance, job, or life to embrace who you truly are and to do what you love? I know for me, once I got that passion to build my business and empower people, it was and is the driving force for me to change things in my life, to create new and better mental and physical habits. I started realizing I had to put myself out there, get over my insecurities, and go after what I really wanted to become. No one was going to give it to me. A change had to happen. I had to be willing, as well to know my limits and see who I could reach out to, to support me in areas that I needed help.

The reality of the situation is that we need to be honest with ourselves. To make the change, we have to replace the lies we are selling and telling ourselves with the truth. Once we find our truth, we have to practice every day application. Often this is the step where people back out or do not last long. Why? When you combine truth with application, it can be quite painful as you make the transition to your authentic self. You know the saying "The truth will set you free". Yes, it will, but it might make life a bit miserable at first.

As I mentioned in previous chapters how learning my "dream job" was not my lifetime job, that was some pretty tough truth to swallow. The change did make me miserable but not for long. I soon found my path, but that first deep look at truth in my life was not pretty but needed.

I worked for many companies as the person who brought in changes to the culture of the company. No matter how good you are at implementing change, people do not like change. Period. It's very much in human nature to resist change. When you are making a change, this feeling of resisting is natural and normal. If you want to embrace your authentic self, you have to be willing to be uncomfortable for a little while. We talk about building good habits in this chapter that helps make change happen. Here is your first challenge. Make it a habit to write down what you want to do. Studies show that if you write down your goals, vision, and plan, you are 90% more likely to complete them.

Nothing is more fun than looking back at our journal of goals and seeing accomplishments!

Once again, you have to find your tribe and not be afraid to reach out for help when needed. Early in my life, I really did not have a great group of people I could turn to for help. In fact, I was pretty solo much of my career, which was difficult. When my mom died, I realized I needed friends I could confide in, talk about the good and the bad, and the tough stuff. I look back now, and I am so glad I created those friendships. They are my second family. Go and find your support group. You can do this by reaching out to friends about being mentors, finding groups that meet on your topic or areas you need help in, and you can research as well what support is out there for your need.

What are the steps to implementing change? Our self-concept is how we view ourselves. It is very unhealthy when we view ourselves in a negative manner. You know the simple saying, garbage in, garbage out? This is exactly the same as our mental self-concept. If we believe we are fat and unintelligent, then we behave this way. To make lasting change, we have to change our self-concept of how we view ourselves.

One of my favorite movies is *What About Bob?* In this movie, the character Dr. Leo Marvin is about to launch his new book called *Baby Steps*. One of his patients, Bob, is afraid of so many things that he gives him his book. This book helps Bob *baby step* his way out of his fears, of course in a very comical way. My point is that baby steps are usually how you want to start. Should you go out and quit your job tomorrow? This is probably not a good idea. If you are reading this and you are having this epiphany as I did, how did I leave this industry and move into another? I took 3 months to plan my exit strategy. I didn't just walk in and quit. I had a family, a newborn, and I was attempting to see how I could make sure I had healthcare and the money to take care of my family. Every case is different, but if you're thinking, in the same way I was, ask yourself, what is your exit strategy to what you are currently doing?

The first step is an exit strategy. Not all of us have the luxury of just quitting our jobs, starting a new business, and not worrying about money. You may have to do what I did, work part-time for a company while running my business until it gets large enough to move to that full time. Maybe the new industry you want to go into requires some certification. While you are at your current job, complete those certifications and get a job lined up to exit from one to the next. Preparation and planning are critical. An exit strategy is recomended to making the change and taking the first step.

Once you have an exit strategy in place and you have progressed to a place where you think your authentic self should be, you are ready for the next steps. You should create a 6-month, 1 year, 3 years, and 5-year plan. Putting a plan in place is imperative to hold you accountable for your new changes. This is a great way to guide you on your path. Often this planning may need to be done with a husband, wife, significant other, or family member to help give you perspective on what you really can do.

Making sure that your family is part of this plan is important: why? As we jump into this New You, it can be very exciting and often we might forget how this change affects our family and those around us. It is imperative that our husband, wife, significant others, and children are a big part of this change. You need their support. If you don't have their support, this change could be very difficult. I have had women say,

> "You're so lucky your husband supports you. Mine does not want to have anything to do with my change or path."

Often, these women's change did not happen, or their business eventually failed because they did not have the support of those in their sphere of influence. Support is *essential* in change. Think about Alcoholics Anonymous (AA): to change and stop the addictive behavior, addicts must follow a 12 step process, to make sure the alcoholic has the support and an accountability partner to go to when things get tough and to hold them accountable. It takes a village to support change. You cannot go it alone.

The next step is an accountability partner. As you make these changes, it gets tough. You will have moments where you want to throw in the towel and go back to what you are familiar with and what you know. This behavior is stronger in the beginning when you try to change. This is where the accountability partner comes in. They help hold you accountable, to encourage you, to help push you to keep going. It's not always easy to find this person, but it is imperative to your continued success to have that accountability partner by your side to support you. I am very lucky that my husband is my accountability partner and my biggest fan. I am as well his biggest fan and accountability partner too. But often I hear from friends that spouses or significant others are not always great for such a partnership; you may need to reach farther out to other friends.

Now is the big moment; time to take those baby steps into moving and changing into your authentic self and start down your authentic path. To be honest, this part of the journey can be such a frightening moment. When I took my first step, questions buzzed through my head. I thought, "*Will I make it or will this just be a big flop in my life? Do I have the grit and determination to do this? What will my family and friends think?*" But you will never be able to answer any of those questions without taking your first step. It is amazing how fear can stop you in your tracks.

I taught speech at the college level for years. People were so afraid to speak in front of others, they would prefer to take a F in the class, than try. I learned I had to create a way to minimize the fear and get them comfortable first. It took time, but I gained their trust, which then made it easier for them to present a speech.

Maybe your first step is making an exit plan of what you want, maybe that business you have been thinking about. Perhaps the first step is to get your business license. Opening a bank account could be the first step or as easy as coming up with a name for your business, writing the first couple pages of your book you always wanted to write, or maybe it is taking that trip you promised yourself for 20 years you were going to take. Whatever step you choose, it all starts with that first step. Remember in the previous chapters I talked about the girl who was given the keys to success but wouldn't take the key and put it in the lock of the door to take that first step because she was so fearful of the new future that she preferred to go back to a horrible environment. Fear of the unknown is often more powerful than what you do know. Even if it is bad, predictable behavior is safer. Nothing to risk. Here is my challenge for you: IT'S TIME! Take your first steps to success. It is the toughest one, and as you keep putting one foot in front of the other, each step gets easier and easier as you move to your authentic path and life. You may have felt in the dark about your authentic self, but no longer. Congratulations—you are about to walk into your authentic path and authentic self.

Next, you need to grow. Growth is not something that happens automatically. Growth only happens when you make a commitment. You have *to want to* grow, plan to grow, show an effort to grow, and continue to persist in growth. The process of becoming your authentic self starts with the intent to change. It is your commitment to change that will shape your life. These choices and commitments to change can do two things: (1) they can either define you or (2) destroy you.

How can you grow? When I wanted to be the best volleyball player I could be, I applied the 10,000-hour rule (Malcolm Gladwell). I spent countless hours practicing over and over, and the more I practiced, the more I grew in the sport. The more I researched and watched other people who were better than me, the more I improved. I learned every aspect of the game so I could master it. Change and growth happen with practice. Practicing change leads to growth, and as you grow, you continue by educating yourself.

When making this change in your life, with these new commitments, you will have to let go of old routines or bad habits. Be sure to give yourself a break if you do find yourself going back to bad habits. We are human, and this is all a process. What is important is being able to identify when we are doing this and recommit to that change. Practice makes change happen!

EXERCISE 3.1

Acknowledging first what needs to be changed in your life is usually the toughest part of the change process. No one wants to acknowledge their weaknesses or areas that just are not that great. To move forward, we must; so this exercise may be tough. Take time to write down what changes you need. If you are brave enough, ask a family or friend as well. Just have a conversation about areas they see you are weak in. Sometimes the hardest part is acknowledging, and then you may feel relief because you put it *out there*. Only then, you can address the change. I will continue to mention throughout this book, take baby steps. Change takes time. Be patient. Change will come.

CHAPTER 4

Practice Change

*"Sometimes it's from the deepest pain
comes the most beautiful creation."*

—DR. JULIE DUCHARME

Congratulations! You have decided to make changes in your life. Good for you! But how can we *practice* change in our life? Being a top-level athlete, people often just think it was easy for me; they would say I was a "athletically talented". The truth is those skills were more natural to me than playing the piano, but I *still* had to put in thousands of hours of practicing. What is really amazing is that it takes 30 days to build a habit. These habits I built with sports have stuck with me for a lifetime to include: discipline, time management, grit, courage, never giving up, and perseverance in the face of struggles. The lesson here is that as you make the change to becoming yourself, know it takes practice. It does not happen overnight. The good news is that once you build these good habits, these skills will last a lifetime. In today's world, we want instant gratification, and we have to remember "Rome was not built in a day."

To practice change, you have to look at the schema in your life. Schema is when we perceive and think about others and situations in terms of the ideas we have already formed about them. Very often we change or distort the truth to make it fit our schema. Or in laymen terms, humans are reluctant to change and often will try and twist things to make them *fit* in their life even if it should not be in their life.

I'd like to share a personal example illustrating the power of practicing change in our mindset. I am very body conscious, much more than probably any family member or friend realizes. Often, I obsess about how imperfect my body is. I work hard to find clothes to cover up my imperfect spots. Sometimes I am too embarrassed to wear an outfit that I really want to wear because I wonder what everyone will think if they see that my tummy is not flat or that my skin is not perfect. It's a real struggle for me; one that I deal with daily in my efforts to accept me, my body, and my beauty.

Body image has been a real struggle since I was in high school. I have worked to embrace me, embrace my body as it is, and my looks; I work through that pain of body image issues every day. Making change is never easy; just like implementing a diet. We want to eat healthy, and perhaps lose some weight, but bad habits are hard to break. For example, it's just so much easier to get fast food than to make a healthy meal. And when I am just completely exhausted and done for the day, that is what I do.

If I wanted to move to healthier eating, I could create meal prep on the weekends when I had more time. I could prep several meals for myself during the week, freeze them, and then I have a healthy meal waiting for me every day that I just need to heat up. Easy. Simple. Just a bit of organization and time needed (as well as commitment). This is also a great way to save money. With any new habit, I would need to start consciously changing my weekend routine to involve this change of making time to meal prep. My friends and

I say this all the time, but I haven't quite taken the leap to move in this direction as my weekends always seem to have a million things going on. A short hour out of my day could easily remedy this for my entire week. If *I* want to change, if **you** want to change, **we** often have to make changes that are not always comfortable at first, but they eventually become habit and routine. Change simply needs time for us to adjust to new routines and new habits.

This last summer was a fun summer with my kids. It was endless swimming, beaches, and floating around. It was the best summer yet, requiring me to be in a swimsuit much of the time and around a lot of people, much skinnier than me. I remember just being horrified at the thought of walking around a waterpark all day in a swimsuit with no cover. I was terrified as we got to the waterpark with the kids. As I looked around at all the other imperfect female bodies there, I realized I could get over this negative self-thinking. I could change my mindset and just have fun with my kids, or I could just hide and pretend on the outside that I was ok but be miserable on the inside.

Like many of you, my kids are everything to me. I would sacrifice anything to make sure they have what they need. This sacrifice includes me putting my selfish, insecure wants aside so they can have a good time. This mindset shift was a good thing because it forced me to make a change. It forced me to see outside of my bubble and realize that change, as painful as it was, was needed in my perspective of myself to see my true beauty. Back to the waterpark we went. I decided as tough as it was, I wasn't going to miss out on my kids having a great time. I took a deep breath, took off my swimsuit cover, and did it. And guess what? Nobody looked at me weird or stared. Nobody gasped and said, *"Wow, what's wrong with your body?"* Even my kids did not notice anything. It was only me.

As I worked through my insecurities, my inner beauty emerged as I saw that my insecurities were only *my* insecurities and no one else cared about my not so flat tummy or my flabby butt. It took me having to walk around a park in a swimsuit to get past those body issues. The rest of the summer I actually had a great time running around in my swimsuit not worried about what others thought. Do I still have insecurities and body issues? Of course, I am human. I concluded that in those moments when I feel insecure, I reflect back on that day at the waterpark and how much fun I had just being me and enjoying life. The choice was mine. And when I feel that struggle coming, I look in the mirror and say *"You know what? I look fine!"* and I leave the mirror and move on with my day. This self-talk can be applied in any situation with any struggle. We can *choose* to struggle, or we can *choose* to embrace it. If I want a thinner body, then it is up to me to make a change in my diet and exercise routine. You *can only* make a change if you actually *want* to change. That change has to start with you deciding *to be dedicated* to that change.

When we let the fear of change control us, it can paralyze our lives. I have watched people so fearful of pursuing another job that they would choose to stay in a bad one with an abusive boss for years to avoid risking change. The very idea of change paralyzed them, even if it was a good change. We have to be willing to face our fear of change; we have to change our perspective and ask, *what if?* All the great leaders, all the barrier breakers, all said the same thing; they couldn't be content with where they were, they had to reach their goal, and to do that they had to help people embrace their idea of change to break that barrier. How can you break your barriers to *make* a change, *practice* change, and *embrace* the authentic you?

What are the steps to start practicing your change? As you will see throughout this book, I will repeatedly *say practice makes a change.* I am sure you have heard *practice makes perfect;* in reality, none of us are perfect. Let's not focus on something improbable or impractical, but practice to make a change, that is a reality. I want to give you a list of tips I practice when I focus on changing my mindset to create new good habits.

1. Start your day with positivity. For me, it is taking a bit of time in the morning to drink my coffee and relax for a moment before the morning craziness starts. This moment of reflection helps me focus on what I need to do for my day.

2. My next tip is to celebrate the small things, just like you would the big things. Life is not one big event; it is a series of small events leading up to big events.

3. The next tip is a big thing for me which is to find humor in the midst of the bad situation. I think women and moms are particularly great at this skill because we have to laugh about some of the crazy stuff that happens in our life, especially with children. Laughter helps me deal with the many failures in my life. I found that these were all lessons in what I needed to do differently. Change those failures into lessons. Don't sit and sulk in the corner because you failed. Get back up, dust yourself off, and figure out how can you be better next time.

4. The next tip is one that I am guilty of, which is getting rid of negative self-talk. I found that I had to really work hard to get negative self-talk out of my life when my daughter was born. I realized anything I said she would internalize. If I said I was fat, then she would look at me and think, well am I fat? I realized I needed to only use positive talk, especially about my body, self-worth, etc. Positivity is contagious; negativity is as well.

5. The next tip is to focus on the present; don't keep revisiting the past or issues from the past. The goal is to create your authentic self, and that means pressing forward. If you linger on negative past events, this focus will hinder your work on practicing change.

6. Make sure to surround yourself with positive friends and family. Negativity is contagious. You may need to distance yourself from these Negative Nellies. You will find that when you are around people who believe in you, support you, and are your biggest fans, making a change and moving to success becomes so much easier. Get the naysayers out of your life, and fast!

7. Finally, I want to talk about not just positive talk, but positive imagery and vision boards. Why? As an athlete, I used to sit and spend time with my eyes closed, imaging me hitting the ball, blocking the ball, and winning the game. I would play these visions in my head over and over, especially after a difficult practice or a bad game. I know, maybe this sounds silly, but ask any high-level athlete if they do this, I bet many will say yes. What does this do? I am training my mind (brain) how to react in those situations and how I need to approach plays. Does

it work? Yes! The mind cannot distinguish between imagination and reality. Practice is practice (plus lots of prayers help as well!). I may not be an active practicing athlete where I spend hours a day practicing my craft anymore, but I still take time visualizing myself practicing a variety of positive things to make a difference. You have to take time to visualize what you want your future to look like. I have, and some have come true; I believe those other goals will as well.

Even if you are a natural at what you do, you still need to sharpen your skills. What type of exercise can we do to strengthen and practice a change in your life to move you to your authentic self? Let me share something I had to do when I working on my self-worth. Often, I feel inadequate with my body, and I had to start just looking at myself in the mirror and saying, "*Julie, you have worth, you are loved, and you are beautiful.*" I know for me this role-playing and mantra was tough, and I thought slightly cheesy, but I realized the more I said these words, the more I believed it. Every time I thought about something bad about myself, I made myself say something I liked about myself. Each one of you are unique, you need to be creative in what you think will help you change your mentality. What I have shared works for me, but maybe for you—you may like to meditate or run, whatever your interest, get involved in a positive group to help you change, be sure to find what makes you flourish so you can practice change.

EXERCISE 4.1

Identify areas in your life that might hold you back from becoming the authentic person you want to be. Know your weaknesses and be honest about them. Next, decide how to deal decisively with them. What is a required change to move to your authentic you? Is it that you need to change your perspective on yourself or your world? Is there a physical thing that needs to change in your routine or life? Once you list these changes, the next step is to focus on how you implement them. Find an accountability partner with whom you can share these changes you want to make with and ask for their help in staying consistent. How can he/she hold you accountable for acting on making these changes day in and day out?

CHAPTER 5

Owning Your Power

What you are is God's Gift to you;
what you do with yourself is your gift to God.

—DANISH PROVERB

I was reading Sheryl Sandberg's book *Lean In,* which is a fantastic book. I had this favorite part I read that I am sure she wrote with a bit of sarcasm, she said,

> "So all a woman has to do is ignore society's expectation, be ambitious, sit at the table, work hard, and then it's smooth sailing all the way."

I love this quote because this is what is expected of all of us women, at least by society's standards. And we women take it is so seriously we find ourselves failing to unrealistic expectations. I attempted to achieve this list of expectations and as good as it sounds there is no smooth sailing. Often, society sets this standard and expectation for women, and it really is an expectation that just sets women up for failure because their expectation is built on male behavior and masculine leadership styles. These expectations are not a realistic expectation of women because we are different in how we work. Is that bad? No, not at all. It's different, and society is so used to these expectations that when someone comes in that is different we have that fear of change.

As I talked about earlier, change is not something people like, even if its good change. So when you are attempting to own your own power, how will YOU shape your power and own it? How *you* define *you* determines your power and how you own it. If you see yourself as a servant, then you may own your power of serving people. If you see yourself as a leader, then you may own the power of leading. One of the best ways I figure people out is by asking them how they see their life. I ask them when they picture life to describe it. Their words and perspective say it all.

Have you ever tried to do something that you just were not good at? If you are an engineer, you would not try to be a medical doctor, right? That is like trying to fit a square peg into a round hole. Why frustrate yourself doing something you are not good at or that does not fit who you are? You are wasting your talent, energy, and time. If we own our own power and discover how to use this power to grow, learn, and shape ourselves, then we will be able to embrace our authentic self fully, as well our full potential as a person. Do not let another day go by without finding and owning your true power. This will help drive your goals, priorities, relationships, and values.

I remember when working for a small college and I was the only woman instructor. I seemed always to get the worst classes and the worst schedules. I couldn't figure out why. I noticed all the male instructors once a week would get together, bring cigars and smoke cigars outside and hang out. I, of course, didn't smoke and so naturally I didn't participate. I realized walking by one day they were talking about schedules. The chair of the program smoked the cigars with them as well, and it dawned on me that he would just do the scheduling right there and I was just getting the leftovers. I decided I was not going to be left out anymore and one day sat down and said,

"Do you mind if I join you?"

They all said I was welcome and offered me a cigar. I declined saying no thank you, but sat in the cigar circle, sucking in second-hand smoke for months, basically being one of the guys and fitting in so I could get the good classes. I thought I had to be one of the guys to be accepted. I was so afraid to speak up to the chair and just ask for my classes. Now I look at this in hindsight and think how ridiculous my behavior was because I did not own my own power. I did get the good classes but at the expense of my health. I was a well-established professor who had excellent credentials and was loved by the college, students, and faculty. I should have just let the Chair know my schedule and what I would like to teach. Instead, I was so caught up in trying to be accepted and be one of the guys, instead of realizing I had power being the only woman there. I had the angle none of them had. I knew how to deal with female students; male faculty often came to me and asked advice on how to approach them or deal with them.

Often as women, we do not own our power. In fact, we very often don't advertise our skills, and we downplay them. We are overly humble and think if we show confidence in our authentic abilities that this confidence is a negative thing. This behavior is so far from the truth. Men have no problem owning their own power and letting you know about it. Very often men will proudly tell you what they are good at and will never take on jobs in which they are not good at. By contrast, women will not tell others what they are good at, and often they will be willing to take on jobs they may not know exactly how to do. As much as women want to fit in, we have to be true to what works best for us. Owning our own power is crucial in becoming our authentic self.

This is where you take a long honest look at what you're really good at and what you're not. In the past, I thought and tried to be the best at everything, but that is not realistic. We all have God-given talents, and we are not meant to be the best at everything. If you struggle with this self-discovery, ask some friends or family. Let them know you really want a true answer, not a compliment. Very often your abilities can be confirmed by friends and family.

Another good way to confirm how you can own your own power is to ask yourself, *"Where have I seen positive growth in my life that other people can confirm as well?"* As we get older, often we embrace more powers than we own. For example, I love to give, I am a leader, and I am an entrepreneur. These are three areas I am very strong in, but when I was younger, I did not own all these areas. Can you grow into some of these areas? Of course!

Look first at what you are currently doing and don't be afraid to look at what you want to be doing later in life. Now if you really can't find your power to own and are not sure, then start experimenting. Get involved in different groups or areas and see what emerges. Maybe you are actually a great leader but just have not yet had the chance to lead. Many years ago, when I was trying to find the right place for me, someone recommended to look carefully at who I was, the work I had done to immerse myself in, what I was great at and loved to do.

When we know our power and how to own it, we can make great change and strides in our lives, the lives of others, and within the lives of our friends and family. One of the powers I own is that I love to help people succeed in finding jobs and live a more fulfilling life; the power of giving. I find such satisfaction in helping others find their way, and I am really good at it! But for a long time, I always sat in the back; I had the answers, but never shared them. I was worried and fearful of what people would say. Maybe they would think I was too cocky, or maybe they didn't want my advice, or maybe they would get offended if I shared what I really thought might be a successful solution as it might go against what they thought. When I finally realized that I wanted to be heard and should be heard, I started owning my own power. I started sitting at the front of the table. I raised my hand high when they asked for a suggestion and spoke eloquently regarding my thoughts. I made sure to acknowledge my colleague's thoughts and say things like

"Let me add to what you are mentioning..."

These steps helped me own my own power, become more respected for my opinion, and made others stand up and take notice of me for my ideas and thoughts. It took a little courage and practice before I stepped up, but I did. When I started owning my own power, that is when I was able to embrace my business, stepped into bigger leadership positions, and saw these areas of my life begin to flourish. When I embraced my power, embraced the change, and embraced my authentic self, I found my new path.

When you find your own power and are ready to own it, take time to enjoy it. Celebrate all wins—big and small. I love helping people and take great joy in owning this power. It is ok to love something you are good at. It's ok to enjoy being good at it. Make the most of your talents and strengths. As with any good garden, we have to work on cultivating what is planted. Sometimes plants need to be pruned to grow bigger and stronger. Sometimes a weed grows and tries to choke out that plant and that weed has to be pulled so the plants can stay healthy. Now that you know your power and the importance of owning your power, you need to make sure you exercise it and keep it strong.

EXERCISE 5.1

What is your power? How can you own your power? Write down a list of your powers. Then write down how you are using or not using them. How can you increase owning your power? If you do not own your power at all, how can you start to own it? It is just like embracing change. How can you move from hiding in that corner like I was to own your power actively? We must take the first step (remember, baby steps!) to make any change; it is same with owning your power. Maybe your power is giving, and you start once a week for 2 hours volunteering at a homeless shelter or helping at a clinic. Owning your own power does not have to be some giant change. Owning your power can be done for the smallest or biggest things in your life. But to be your authentic self, you need to own your power.

CHAPTER 6

Worth

No matter what I say, what I believe,
I am bankrupt without love.

—1 CORINTHIANS 13:3

You are not an accident. Your life is not a mistake. Your birth was not a mishap or accident. You are meant to be here on this earth. I truly believe God choose you to be here. Life is about love. The most important lesson you can learn on this earth is learning to love yourself as you are. Learning to love yourself unselfishly is a tough task. It's tough just to love other people, but to accept yourself fully, that you are a wonderful person who deserves to be loved, that seems to be tough for everyone to do.

My favorite verse to read when I feel like I am not worthy is Isaiah 44:2 "I am your creator. You were in my care even before you were born." The thought that I am a special creation of the almighty God and that I was created for a purpose in this big world reminds me of how special I really am. Knowing I am not an accident changed my perspective on my worth. Whether you believe in God or not, one thing I can tell you is that you are not an accident; you are a beautiful, unique person who has a special purpose in this world.

We all have weaknesses, as well as imperfections to include physical, emotional, intellectual, and spiritual issues.

You could also have other situations in your life weakening you as well such as financial hardships or relationship issues. What is even more important is how we look at these issues to deal with them to learn how they affect our view of our worth. Often, people will find ways to hide these issues with excuses, depression, and a long list of other issues that arise from not dealing and acknowledging that we are not perfect, but we are worthy. We have to learn our attributes and how to use them. Regularly, we try to become or embody attributes that are not true to who we are and then we face the disappointment of why we couldn't be just like that other person. There is nothing wrong with acknowledging our weaknesses and either working to strengthen them or realizing maybe we need help in those areas. When we acknowledge that we can't do everything, (and it's ok not to be the best at everything), it can help us learn how to embrace our strengths and thrive.

Let me give an example. I used to try to be the best at everything and thought I had to, or I wasn't a strong, successful woman. I realized I couldn't do everything, and it was ok to ask for help. Once I started acknowledging that I needed help, life didn't seem so overwhelming. I also had to be willing to acknowledge to people like my husband that I needed help. I didn't like to do that as I worried he would think I couldn't handle myself as a mother, wife, and woman. This realization was so the opposite. I needed to communicate to him my needs because we were a team and I needed my teammate. When I started communicating with him, we became a strong team, and we started dominating in many great things in our life such as in our business and our relationship. When we were both able to say,

"I am not great at this, could you help me?"

We knew each other's strengths, and we could help each other. It is amazing how we took so much pressure off each other. In those moments, we owned our own power because we realized our strengths and weaknesses. One of the biggest failures of women is not realizing their strengths and owning them. Instead, we always like to identify our weaknesses and focus on those instead of our own power and how we can use that to make a change and be who God truly called us to be. I found some statistics that really reveal how women are valuing themselves.

When I looked at the recent statistics of suicide in our nation in 2015, it confirmed my worst fears about how women especially feel about their worth. The Centers for Disease Control and Prevention (2015) reported:

Suicide was the tenth leading cause of death for all ages in 2013. There were 41,149 suicides in 2013 in the United States—a rate of 12.6 per 100,000 is equal to 113 suicides each day or one every 13 minutes a person dies from suicides. Among students in grades 9-12 in the U.S. during 2013, 17.0% of students seriously considered attempting suicide in the previous 12 months (22.4% of females and 11.6% of males), 13.6% of students planned about how they would attempt suicide in the previous 12 months (16.9% of females and 10.3% of males). 8.0% of students attempted suicide one or more times in the previous 12 months (10.6% of females and 5.4% of males). 2.7% of students made a suicide attempt that resulted in an injury, poisoning, or an overdose that required medical attention (3.6% of females and 1.8% of males).

There are many more statistics I could add. When looking at these numbers, I noticed that the females are the highest in every stat of people with suicidal thoughts, attempts, and finally killing themselves. This information confirms my belief that women do not know their worth.

Our society promotes a woman's worth as being skinny, sexy, wearing, the right clothes, dating the right person, and having the perfect family; the list goes on and on. Social media compounds this stereotype as people are painting a picture—a perfect life for themselves with edited pictures. Society says this is what your authentic self *should* look like and sound like. You will not see anyone posts about their depression, anxiety, feelings of lacking, or even suicidal thoughts. They will post their perfect edited pictures to fit in. As women, we seek to meet these standards so we can feel accepted, loved, and meet the expectations of society. Sadly, no matter how skinny you are, how pretty you make yourself, or how perfect you try and make your life, it means nothing, if you do not love who you are as a person.

I reflected recently about some very high profile suicides from some recent celebrities. I remember their loved ones talked about their success and how shocked they were that this happened because they were so successful. How could they not be happy? This was a resounding theme in each of these articles. Family and friends couldn't understand it. But people were measuring what they considered success-ful in their lifespan as society's idea of success and worth, not looking at the person's true authentic self. When you embrace you, the good and the bad, we feel a fulfillment. Pretending to be something other than your authentic self is quite exhausting.

Has anyone ever asked you what your worth is? I don't think anyone has ever asked me what my worth was. I never thought about what I was worth. I just always thought about how I did not measure up. When I was in high school, I remember the mean girls pointed out that my breasts were not big enough, I didn't have the right shoes, or my hair wasn't the right look. They made sure I felt as bad as I could about myself. Thank God for my Mother. She was a bird who flew to her own music. She didn't care what she wore, and if she fit in with the other mothers; she didn't care if other people loved it, she just cared that *she* loved it. She always pushed me to be myself, *always*. She saw my worth so clear; she used to tell me that I would change the world and God made me for a special reason.

As I look back on those moments, I realize that I want every girl and woman to know they were made with a special purpose and their worth is priceless. I want them to be comfortable being them. I love to be silly, funny, and wear super baggy clothes. I love not to wear makeup and just be a mess some days. But for so long, I never felt comfortable looking at being like that. All the women around me were so put together, and I thought I needed to look totally put together (even if I wasn't put together on the inside!), and so I was always making sure I had makeup on, the best brand named clothes I could afford, (and sometimes not afford, but bought them anyway!). I realized that I wanted people to like me whether I had makeup on or not, whether I was a little heavier than I was 10 years ago, and if I wasn't wearing the perfect outfit, they still loved me. The question is, how do we get past this? How do we learn our worth and make changes to embrace our authentic selves?

If you asked me who I was when I was younger, there was a good chance I would not have had an answer for you. If you ask me today, I would say I am a unique special creation; that is what we all are. But society and culture dictate so many negative messages. The world we live in encourages us in our moments of confusion to just not be anyone. You don't want to be a man or a woman; just be nothing. I can't imagine how it would feel to deny ourselves who we are, just to be nothing. We are at a point that parents call their kids an *IT*! Could you imagine not having a name or a gender or knowing who you are? The loneliness that must come with not knowing who you are must be overwhelming.

When I picked out the names for my children, I made sure their names had a meaning that gave them purpose as a person. My daughter, Abigail's name has several meanings, depending on what language you pick. One of the meanings is princess warrior. As I reflected on this meaning, I knew my daughter in this day and age would need to be a warrior to make it in this tough world. I like the princess part because I wanted her to know she could embrace being a girl and still be a warrior. I wanted her to know she could be a woman and be strong to know this power would not diminish her. I know it may sound pretty intense how I picked her name, but I wanted her to know the strength that comes from being her authentic self. She has embraced her princess warrior name quite well thus far!

My son, Micah's name, means messenger of God. I loved this name because being a messenger of the people is an important task in a world that delivers such despicable information. When Micah was younger, he would talk at home but not much at the school. The school started to make a big deal about it. I took him to the doctor, even though I knew in my heart he was fine. The doctor said he was fine but sent him for a test to put my mind at ease. The ear doctor, eye doctor, and speech therapist all said he was fine, but yet I was still harassed by the school that there just must be something wrong with him. I kept trusting my heart and my mom intuition. I knew I gave him the name for a reason. Maybe 6 months after this, Micah started bursting with words and started talking at school; so much so now I have to ask him to take a breath so I can get a word in otherwise. My point in sharing this is that the world insisted because he wasn't speaking like another child that there was something wrong with him. Yet it was the opposite. Micah was just being Micah. He was growing into his personality, but yet the world was insisting he wasn't like the other kids and there was something wrong with him. This is exactly how it happens for us as we grow up and even as adults. The world sees different and does not like it; the world says you must be like us to be accepted. When we measure ourselves by societal standards, we will never win. We will always fall short because the world's standards are not realistic and can never be met. When you truly examine your life, make a change, practice change, and own your power to know your worth, you will be unstoppable in embracing your authentic self.

Here is a good question to ask yourself. When we are young, people would ask

"What do you want to be when you grow up?"

In our reply, we might say things like policeman, firefighter, doctor, astronaut, and so many other things because they look like such an exciting profession. My son has a new career he wants to do every day, and so does my daughter. Even though some things they say they want to do often seem not remotely attainable, knowing the depths and lengths of what has to happen to get to that job, I still let them dream. I don't tell them it's not possible, because when you dream about what you really want your authentic self to be, then barriers are just a mere speed bump in the road.

We ask our high school students to pick their profession for life at age 18 and go to college. By age 21, the expectation is to be working in the dream job. It's one of the most unrealistic, and unfair things we do to kids. What we want to do at 18 is very often not what we want to do at 25 or 30 or beyond. I was pushed to be an English teacher; I was told that's a good job for women. I remember thinking "*I can't stand teaching,*" let alone teaching kids, and English is not my thing. I kept being conditioned in my schools to look at that as a profession. I was deterred more than once being told teaching was a good profession for women. There is nothing wrong with teaching; it just was not my passion. I fought against what the world told me *I should* do and what I wanted to do. Society will attempt to condition you to what they think you *should* be, but society can never know your true self-worth, and what you were meant to do, only you can *choose* that.

I share these thoughts with you because who you are is not just defined by your job; it is an essential part of who you are but it does not define you. Who am I? I am a mother, wife, business owner, women empowerment speaker, and so much more. I knew I didn't want to be defined by just one thing as I had so much more to offer.

I pose the question again, who do you want to be? If I were to ask some of you who you were and what did you do, what would you say? I know at the end of the day; I want to be someone whose life made a difference. This is much different than what I thought I wanted to do at age 18. As I said earlier, to find your authentic self, you have to know your worth. But you can't find your worth in things society says; you can only know your true worth by embracing you and your own power. If you are feeling hopeless, don't. Wonderful changes will happen in your life by making a change to your authentic self.

EXERCISE 6.1

If your self-concept is getting in the way of your thinking and how you see your worth, then you need to practice letting go of those false and negative ideas you have of yourself. Letting go of these false ideas of you is key to knowing your worth. Work on the following list below to start to change your self-concept.

- List traits you most admire about yourself. Then list the trait you want to embody but do not currenlty have?

- How can you apply these traits to change how you view your worth?

- What changes do you need to make in your life to feel positive about your worth?

CHAPTER 7
Engage

What drives you in your life? What makes you engage in what you are doing? Often we are driven by stress, problems, pressure, or deadlines, but these are the things that make us engage in life. Knowing your purpose of what you want to change in your life is what gives you meaning to engage. You have taken a deep look at yourself; you have talked about the change, practiced the change, and now you are going to engage in the change actively. You are going to start incorporating this into your life with friends, family, and work.

Another important part of changing something in your life is having hope. Hope is so important for your life. Why? Because you may feel like a failure when you continue to struggle as you work to make change. It is important to know you have hope; hope helps you know that you are moving in the right direction.

Who we are is how we think. Your upbringing may dictate whether you are positive, negative, conservative, or liberal, etc. Our upbringing can shape the way we think, as well as create our fears, and affect the way we think and engage with the world. It can shape our confidence, our self-concept, and our emotions. This requires that we continue to honestly look at how we can be our authentic self. We must face these barriers to know who we really are and want to be.

When we practice change, we also have to take it to the next level to engage our new authentic self. Often times, this change can be nerve-wracking to think, *"Oh you want me to go out in front of other people and actually be my authentic self? Wait! Hold up; maybe I'll just keep practicing at home."* Part of becoming who you are is to actutally engage with friends and family. If you want to be a business owner, take business courses, get your business license, but if you never take the step to *start* the business, then you have not moved from practicing being your authentic self to engaging in being your authentic self.

I have met many women who say to me,

"Well I really want to do this, but I just don't know how it works."

My response usually is,

"Well, research it and find out, then you can make your decision."

It is amazing to me how many women will not take the extra step to find out and do additional research. They love to *practice,* but they do not want to *engage,* because engagement can often be very scary for many people. Engagement means you have taken the next step to becoming authentically you. It is the final step needed to accept you and embrace you. Remember the first exercise we did in chapter 1 about what barriers are holding you back from doing the things you love or being the person you want to be? This is where many women stop the process; those barriers come back, whether fear, time, money, or something else, it comes back, and so do the excuses.

Remember our talk earlier in the book about the *Biggest Loser* and the pain that often comes hand-in-hand with the beautiful change we are making in our lives? This is the biggest and most difficult step you will take to become authentically you because it's time to test you. Embracing who you are is a terrifying thing because you do not know if you will be accepted by family, friends, and society. Who will mock you, who will tell you it's wrong, you're not good enough, or that you shouldn't be you cause it's too different? If you can take this next step, this is where you will truly see freedom from the hold the world and society have on you.

Remember my Mom and how I talked about her earlier in this book. Only when she was dying did I see how her true beauty and her zest for embracing who she was, left her with no regrets, how even though her life was shorter than we all planned, she left in peace, freedom, and joy because she lived a life of being authentically her. Now is *your* time to start actively engaging in what you have been practicing and put that practice into action. Your journey may start with baby steps, as not everyone can jump head first into change, but taking the first step to move you from practice to engagement is what you need. Are you ready to engage?

EXERCISE 7.1

For this exercise, it is time to pick your first engagement to become authentically you. If you remember in the previous exercises, you were told to find an accountability partner to help you make a change. Now it is time to go back to that accountability partner and talk about the first step(s) you are going to take to move from *practicing* to *engaging*. A good example I often hear women say is that they want to be a speaker. I encourage them to join a group that supports speakers; consider the national group called *ToastMasters*. You get to meet with this group on a regular basis and practice your talks. It's a great way to get started. Using this type of example, how can you take your first steps? Share with your accountability partner what you plan to do, put a plan in place, mark a date on the calendar, and ask them to come along to support you on the sidelines.

CHAPTER 8

Reflection

People have been trying to figure out their purpose in life since the beginning of time. They want fulfillment, purpose, and happiness. When we ask ourselves questions like what do I want to be? Or what should I do with my life? That answer for many of us was right in front of us all along; we were simply missing the blinking sign. In life, we have to constantly reflect on what we are doing and how we are living our lives. Have you ever started out so passionate about something, a dream you were following, and suddenly you are looking at your life thinking how did I get here? This is not where I want to be? How did I lose my vision, my passion, and my dreams? You are not alone. I have talked to countless women asking these questions and then asking themselves, how do I get back to that? Now they have jobs, families, and responsibilities and those dreams they held once upon a time, seem so distant and unachievable.

Balance is a very important aspect when we reflect. In anything we do in life, big or small changes, we have to real-istically look at what we can and can't do in our lives. The world puts so many expectations on our lives. As mentioned earlier, I was so hard on myself to be that perfect woman and found nothing but failure because I had to realize no one was perfect and I needed balance in my life. There is nothing more powerful than a focused life that has purpose. People who made a difference in history all had focus, balance, and purpose.

When you begin to reflect on your next steps, the final piece to making change and becoming authentically you is forgiveness and healing. A major change in your life can't happen without the forgiveness of a person or perhaps even yourself. Healing and change can't happen unless we forgive. The first chapter in this book I talk about the person who told me I wasn't smart enough. More than 10 years later, I forgave him, ended up at his grandkids' parties, and attended his funeral.

Each time I forgave people who hurt me deeply, it helped me move forward. Often, we don't realize how we harbor anger, resentment, and so much more that doesn't serve us—we don't reflect on our pain. Honestly, none of us want to think about the pain in our lives. But it is often necessary to pull off that band-aid and take a look at the wound. You might be thinking, *"Julie, I can't forgive a person for what they did to me or I don't know how to forgive myself."* If you want to move forward to being your authentic self, then you have to take this next step of reflecting back on what you need to do to forgive, to heal to move forward. It takes time. The person I talk about above took me 10 years to complete the forgiveness process. I can't believe I held that grudge for that long. I am a little embarrassed to admit, but they hurt me deeply and I did not know how to let that go. I was very young, and I didn't know at that time in my life how to process the hurt.

Following your Dreams

My husband and I love the beach. We fell in love with a beautiful family friendly beach town in San Diego, CA. One problem that existed is that these beautiful beach town-homes were nothing less than a $1 million dollars plus. Every time we would come to the beach, we would talk about how amazing it would be to live by the beach; we dreamed some day of owning a home and being able to walk to the beach with our kids and raising them in this cute town. It seemed like a dream that would never happen for a small business owner/professor and an elementary school teacher.

Finally, one day I thought, I am just going to start looking at places and put my dream into perspective. I first started looking at open houses and places for rent (baby steps). Then I brought my hubby along. While we were looking (and dreaming!), at some point we asked,

"What we could do is start first by renting, as we could afford that while we save up to buy, right?"

Then my husband said, "Well, you would have to make more money."

I said, "Ok, I could do that."

I went back to my businesses and started to re-engineer them to expand. Suddenly, I realized that the only limit in me making money was me. About 6 months after that conversation, we were moving to our favorite beach town, and not to some tiny little apartment which is what we originally thought we could afford, but to a beautiful home on the water.

I share this story not brag but to show you the possibilities that can happen if you have the right mindset. If I had listened to everyone who thought this was a crazy idea and didn't think we had the money, I would have just said "You're right," and we would still be in our old home. Being the dreamer I am, I didn't want to wait until I was retiring to live at the beach. We have been here in this house 4 years as of this writing; my business is thriving because I was willing to change my perspective as I was only limited by my thought that I was as a "small business" and had to stay that way. In the end, I always possessed the skills and ideas to move my business to the next level, but needed the motivation to see that I could do it.

I was told for so long that women couldn't and shouldn't *do business* that I limited myself to what I thought I could make without realizing I was doing this. Once I embraced myself as a strong, educated business woman who knew how to make money, I then started making my dreams come true and behaving like my true authentic self. When you apply the empower method—**E**xamine, **M**ake a change, **P**ractice change, **O**wn your power, and **R**eflect on all of this, you can see how to move beyond these limiting beliefs to be your authentic self. Success will enter your life as you begin living your true authentic path and life. You may have been in the dark about who you were in the past, but **CONGRATULATIONS!** You are now walking into your authentic self and life.

EXERCISE 8.1

Reflect on what your perspectives were at the beginning of this book and what your perspectives are now? What changes have you made or are willing to make to move to a more authentic you?

DAY 1

It might be a bit cliché, but today is the first day of the rest of your life. Yes, it is. You are taking the first step in making changes in your life. Today we are taking our first baby step. I want you to journal, what is the first step you are taking today? Write down your first step and ask yourself, why is this your first step to change? It's time to write it all down TODAY!! Not tomorrow, not when you get to it. TODAY!

Today is change Day 1.

DAY 2

Just like a New Year's Resolution, we are excited! It's only Day 2—you can do this. Excitement is in the air and you are ready!!! Remember you are responsible for your attitude. Attitude affects everything we do. No one thing or person can make you happy or make you change. You have to have the attitude that you want change.

Journal today on these changes:

DAY 3

Today is Day 3. You might start to feel a twinge and that is ok; depending on the changes in your life, you could be feeling a roller coaster of emotions. For example, if you were a drug addict or addicted to something similar, you would start to exhibit withdrawal symptoms at this point. When we are not getting nourished over and over with what we are used to getting, we start to feel those symptoms of withdrawal. Yes, this is normal. Your body and/or your mind is craving for those negative habits or lifestyle you have lived with for so long. You have to decide what are your "bad" areas and how will you adjust your attitude towards those bad areas.

DAY 4

Today is Day 4. Let's imagine you are on a diet and that body is really craving all that sugar you used to put in it. Oh, didn't those yummy treats taste so good and make you feel so good?!? Until the sugar crash that is. Then, to get rid you of that feeling, you ate more sweets and even more sweets, because you did not like that low feeling, the feeling was just plain yucky. But as long as you could be on that sugar high, life was good. But the "sugar highs" of life only last so long. If you want to see change, you need to behave, act, and even speak like the person you want to be.

Journal about the person you want to be.

DAY 5

Wahoo!!! It's Day 5! You have made it the length of a work week. Congratulations! Today, I want you to answer these questions. How is the change going? What do I need to do next to keep moving in the right direction? Am I moving too fast and need to slow down and do more baby steps? Or am I doing really well, and I can move to some bigger changes? These are key questions to ask yourself as you are coming up on almost a week in the change process. Do we backtrack sometimes? Yes, it's normal. If you back tracked a bit, then go back to your Day 1 change and do that again. Finally, be sure to ask yourself, how are you managing your attitude towards all of this? Is an attitude adjustment needed?

DAY 6

If you are just breezing through this first week, *good for you!* If this was a super tough week for you, don't worry, it will get easier. Remember, you are retraining your brain to think differently. Changing behaviors is tough but changing destructive or abusive behaviors is very tough. One of the most important aspects in change is finding the positive in all you do. Life can be tough, but I can bet if you try you can always find something positive. Know that your attitude often will need a daily adjustment. So, let's check that attitude, how is your attitude affecting your behavior today?

DAY 7

You did it!!! **CONGRATULATIONS**!!! For the first week of making change, big or small, you did it! *Celebrate the small victories just like big victories.* We all work on different levels. It does not matter how small or big your change is; you put in a week of hard work moving towards becoming the authentic you. If this week, all you did was look in the mirror and say *"I am worthy. I can do this,"* you made great strides. If this week, you walked away from an abusive job, friend, or loved one, you made big strides. If this week, you went and obtained your business license to start that amazing business idea you have, you made change. Whatever level— **Congrats!!!** You are moving in a great direction. Remember practice brings change. Today, I want you to reflect in your journal about what was tough, what was easy, and what you need to do to keep moving in the right direction for making positive change. Also, talk about what your plan is for next week and what changes you hope to make. If 30 days of change means you look in the mirror for 30 days and say you are worthy, you are making change!

DAY 8

Wow!! You made it through the first week. Give yourself a hand! As I mentioned before, if the first week was tough, but you kept going, this next week will be better, as your mind is now realizing it needs to change. At the beginning of each week, check in with your accountability partner. Let them know how the week went, what you plan to change, and what you plan to do this upcoming week. Once again, this week remember our analogy of rinse, repeat, and review. AND remember, practice makes change.

Write below your goals for change this week and what you plan to do this week.

DAY 9

When you are working hard to build muscle, they say if you are working hard and training right it will take around a couple weeks to build that first pound of muscle. Experts say it takes about 3 months to build 5 pounds. This week I want you to find someone who is always positive and incorporate them into your life, I want you to also create positive conversations with many people and remove negative words from your vocabulary.

Journal about how you are going to do that.

DAY 10

One of my favorite commercials is by Geico—(the insurance company with the famous Gecko!). They are simply the funniest and most memorable commercials on TV. One of their classic commercials that I love is the one with the camel walking around the office as he keeps asking each employee, "Ask me what day it is?" Which of course nobody wants to answer him until finally someone grumbles while rolling their eyes, "What day is it"? And he yells, "It's Hump day!" Guess what? In Week 2, today is . . . Hump Day!! In a regular week, when I get to Wednesday, I think *"Ok! Hump day—two more days to go to get to that weekend!"* You might be feeling like this. Life happens and we have good and bad days. How do we get past hump day? We keep going. Today, review your goal(s) and your plan or "exit strategy" on how you are planning to get there. Often, we need to remind ourselves of our goal. With the goal in mind, things become very clear. No one ever became great at something without having some grit, courage, and persistence. How will you have grit, courage, and persistence this week to move to becoming your authentic self?

DAY 11

I played sports; basketball was a big sport I played, as well as volleyball. One of my all-time favorite basketball players was Michal Jordan. He has a way of defying gravity and making it look so easy and amazing. I remember the critics said he was a one trick pony and he couldn't deliver shooting outside or 3 points. He took on the challenge and started to refine his game. Then out of the blue, here comes Jordan shooting outside and draining 3 pointers like it was nothing. The critics said "Well, the team wouldn't win if you stopped shooting," To answer their comments, the next game he had something like 46 assists, showing he could be a team player and not have to dominate everything by himself. The idea here is that Michael saw where he was deficient and worked to become stronger in those areas; eventually he mastered all parts of the game. He realized that to improve his game, he had to change his mindset, which not only improved his game but bettered his team and the people surrounding him. Today, reflect on how your attitude change is not only benefiting you, but benefiting your family, friends, and community as well. Remember, a rising tide lifts all boats.

DAY 12

When I am struggling with me and having a hard day, often it is easy to get into that deep dark hole of depression. But I have found that this is all attitude and perspective. Often it helps me to express gratitude to others, to help others, to give to others. It is amazing how fast our attitude changes when we help others who are less fortunate than us. So where do you stand when it comes to your attitude of change today? Have you made the decision to make that daily attitude adjustment?

DAY 13

What are your priorities today? When I have a list of items that are very important, I make a list. I put the most important on top and work my way down. How are you making your decisions on what priorities of change need to happen in your life? We have to make deliberate decisions on how we will prioritize the change in our life and how we will create an effective focus on doing this. If you want change to happen in your life, then you have to make the decision to make the change a priority.

DAY 14

You have now hit 2 weeks of working to empower change in your life. I find that reflection is always an important aspect when making change. Reflect today on how the last 2 weeks have gone. Ask yourself questions such as, *What type of return have I received on my change? Has this change been good for me? How can this continued change in mindset and attitude continue to move me in a good direction?*

DAY 15

Often times we live a certain way for so long that we do not realize how detrimental it is in our lives, whether it be mental or physical. When I was in a very hostile work environment, I remember I had my son and at the 8-week mark I was checked out by the doctor and cleared with excellent health. Just a few months after, I was back to see my doctor as my hair was falling out, I was getting urinary tract infections, and having constant chest pain. In just a few months of living in this stress filled environment, I went from excellent health just after having a baby to a possible heart attack victim because of the world I was living in. When we look at the change that needs to happen in our lives, what is our mental health status? How are you working to make healthy attitude changes, healthy decisions, and healthy mental changes? Today, journal about how you are making these adjustments or need to make these adjustments.

DAY 16

What is your purpose for living? I know this is a pretty deep question, but I think often we have to reevaluate our purpose in our life. Why are we doing what we are doing and what changes do we need to make to be sure we are meeting the goals of our purpose? A question I often ask my clients is, *Do you enjoy what you do at work?* If not, why don't you enjoy it? Do you have a plan in place to move to something you do love to do that meets your purpose?

Journal today on how your changes meet your purpose for life and what you are doing to meet those goals, if you are not meeting your purpose.

DAY 17

Any time I meet someone and they ask me what I do, it's always a loaded question because it's never easy to explain how I own and run three companies, remain a college professor, public speaker, and author (*that's the short version*). Their next question is *How do you do all of that?* My response usually is good time management. I always tell people you have to find the right pace for you. I learned early on not everyone can move at my pace, actually very few can. As you make change in your life, know your pace. Next to knowing your pace, as you make your changes, know your self-worth. Lack of self-worth can slow us down, deter us, and mess up our pace. Finally, in the midst of all that is going on, learn to laugh. Sometimes, my day would be so wacky I would think there were cameras hidden, just watching me make a fool of myself. But in the end, I had to look at this crazy day or situation and laugh because that was all I could do. Journal today about what your pace is or you want it to be. How are you affected when your pace does not match you?

DAY 18

As we talked about in this book, when you are making change in your life, you do have to consider family, friends, significant others, and how the change in your life may affect them. As you have been making changes in this 30-day challenge to empower yourself, check in with your family, friends, or significant others and see what they think about the change. Are they noticing it? Is it affecting them in a positive way? Can they be more involved in your change?

Journal about your results.

DAY 19

The mind is a very powerful tool. With positive thoughts and training, we could achieve greatness or we could literally convince ourselves we are sick. People have become so negative to convince themselves that suicide was a better option than life. Our mind is so powerful. That is why positive thinking brings great results. We must train our minds to make good decisions with positive thinking.

As you continue to make change in your life on this 30-day journey, we need to practice daily positive thinking and positive decision thinking. You are more than halfway through your journey of change and this is where self-doubt may come or the fear that this change may really happen and then what? But if we practice positive thinking every day, then we will create positive decisions in our life. As you work on your positive thinking. I want you to pick something positive about your life right now and journal about it. Know that you need to focus on growing your strengths and putting those weaknesses to bed. Stop focusing on your weaknesses and focus on how you can grow those strengths using positive thinking and decision-making.

DAY 20

You are 10 days from finishing this 30-day challenge to empower your change. Right now, our commitment has been strong. Commitment in your life is important and very often, people do not stick to the commitments they make. Often, they flake on family and friends after they have said they will help, be part of an event, or show up for a meeting, and they don't. It is important as you work to empower your change, you also work on deciding to keep your commitment to this change daily. As an athlete, I had to be committed to get up every morning and work out, shoot that basketball every day, hit that volleyball every day. No growth would come without me making a conscious decision to commit to becoming the best player I could be. This is the same here: how do you need to adjust your commitments to empower your change?

Journal about this.

DAY 21

Are you willing to pay the price for what you need to do to empower change in your life? When making change in life, attitude, decisions, thinking, and commitment play such an important part, but the final step is being willing to pay the "price" of what the changes bring. Maybe you decided to stop spending time with friends who have a negative influence on you and the "price" is you need new friends. Maybe you get out of a negative relationship and the "price" is you are lonely for period of time as you figure out where you go next. How willing are you to maintain this change at whatever cost to you?

Journal about this.

DAY 22

As you see change happening in your life, you are going to naturally want to compare yourself to others. The simplest example is weight loss. As the weight comes off, you will naturally compare yourself to other women to see if you are looking like them. We talked about this in the book, if we are always comparing to someone else or society's expectation we will always be disappointed. Remember, you are making these changes for you, not for someone else. If you find yourself comparing yourself to someone else's life, stop. Don't make assumptions and do not try to be like someone else. Embrace your authentic self.

Journal about struggles you have with comparing yourself to others.

DAY 23

As you look back on the last 23 days, I am sure you have observed growth in your life. Big or small, growth is good. As we work to empower our change, growth is something we want to practice daily. We have to make conscious decisions on how we can grow together. As you reflect on your growth, ask yourself: *What is my true potential?* You have made a commitment to change. Now let's set some goals for growth.

Journal about your goals and how you plan to reach those goals.

DAY 24

Yesterday, we discussed growth goals. Today, I want to talk about how you can put yourself in situations and environments to make those growth goals happen. When I was playing sports, I spent as much time as I could in the gym, playing, practicing, and playing pickup games with people much better than me, because I knew? I could learn from them. What environment can you put yourself in to make this growth happen?

Journal about this.

DAY 25

Today our world values seem to have become very skewed. Part of change is practicing good values you can apply to your life and the change(s) you are making. What are your values? How can you incorporate them into your change? What values might need to be altered to empower your change? You have to decide daily to make good decisions about your values.

Journal on this.

DAY 26

Not every day is easy. I can attest to that, but when we implement a good attitude, good decision-making, commitment, growth, goals, and values, we can start to see life align in a better light. If we approach each day by evaluating these areas, reflect and think about how positive behavior consistently affects our lives, we will continue to empower our change You are just a couple days from completing this challenge.

Journal about the six areas mentioned above and out of those six, which ones could use continued work and growth?

DAY 27

There are many types of thinking you can implement in your life. A list includes realistic thinking, reflective thinking, unselfish thinking, and creative thinking. What is your thinking mentality, and does it need alterations to better help the change you are making in your life?

Journal today about your thinking mentality and how this thinking affects your decisions, and if your thinking needs to be modified in order to maintain the changes you've implemented in your life.

DAY 28

You have made many decisions on this 30-day path to empower change in your life. By now, habits should be forming such as changing your mindset, changing your attitudes, and changing your decision-making. Today, I want you to evaluate all of these habit changes mentioned above. What is the most important one you need to work on daily to continue to be successful in your change?

Journal about this.

DAY 29

During this change process, it shows that you decided to improve your life with empowering some type of change. Was that decision hard? How did you conclude you needed change in your life? Reflect back on what started you on this journey. It's important to remind ourselves of why we wanted change, what change we made, and why we want to maintain this change in our lives.

DAY 30

You really can make change in your life! You followed this change plan for 30 days to empower your authentic self. One of the keys to your success is that you made important decisions to make change. You managed those decisions in a positive way with implementing attitude changes, commitment changes, changes in your decision-making, and changes in the way you think. Anyone who follows these strategies consistently can empower change on a regular basis in their life. I want to encourage you to pick a new goal each month to address making good change in your life.

Journal about the goals of change you want to accomplish over the next 6 months and celebrate that you empowered your way to your authentic self.

About the Author

As a change maker, **Dr. Julie Ducharme** has dedicated her career to empower and support people in their endeavors and dreams. People from all over, including the corporate sector and those returning to the workforce, have taken the advice and guidance of Dr. Julie and learned how to use their strengths to maximize their work/life success. Her unique speaking style ignites the passion inside us all and makes that tiny spark into a blaze of empowerment.

Since earning her MBA and Doctorate degrees in business and organizational leadership, Dr. Julie has become a national best-selling author, recognized by *Inc.* magazine; hosts a podcast; appeared on TV numerous times with CBS, ABC, and Fox; and has become a professional public speaker and serial entrepreneur.

Her book *Leading by My Ponytail: Why Can't I Wear Pink and Be the President?* was named by *Inc.* magazine one of the top 60 leadership books for women.